ART OF WAR WISDOM

孫子兵法

ART OF WAR WISDOM

Great Quotes from the Classic Military Treatise

SUN TZU

First published in 2026

Amber Books Ltd
United House
North Road
London N7 9DP
United Kingdom
www.amberbooks.co.uk
Facebook: amberbooks
YouTube: amberbooksltd
Instagram: amberbooksltd
X(Twitter): @amberbooks

ISBN: 978-1-83886-641-9

Translated by James Trapp
Design & Editorial: Amber Books Ltd

Printed and bound in China

TRADITIONAL CHINESE BOOKBINDING
This book has been produced using traditional Chinese bookbinding techniques, using a method that was developed during the Ming Dynasty (1368–1644) and remained in use until the adoption of Western binding techniques in the early 1900s. In traditional Chinese binding, single sheets of paper are printed on one side only, and each sheet is folded in half, with the printed pages on the outside. The book block is then sandwiched between two boards and sewn together through punched holes close to the cut edges of the folded sheets.

Contents

Introduction

It is an unusual book that was written 2500 years ago in an impenetrable classical language and yet is on the reading list of the United States Marine Corps today.

Welcome as it is to see a classical text being preserved not just for its venerable antiquity but also for its contemporary relevance, there are at least a couple of caveats that need to be applied. Firstly, although the historical context of the current accepted version of the text is complex and still open to debate, it seems fairly clear that the core text was composed by one man for, in all likelihood, a specific ruler. There is not much in either practical or theoretical terms in *The Art of War* that can be considered unique, or even particularly innovative. What made the book of such value is that it is likely that it was the first time all its various observations on tactics and attitudes, both general and specific, were gathered together and coordinated.

Secondly, there are a plethora of instances where the principles of *The Art of War* are applied to contemporary circumstances that wish to be seen as a form of modern-day warfare. These range from the obvious, in the world of business; to the absurd, in a book entitled *Golf and the Art of War: How*

the Timeless Strategies of Sun-Tzu Can Transform Your Game. In each context, it must always be recognized that the shift from a beleaguered Bronze Age Chinese kingdom to 21st century business – big or small – completely alters the premises on which the advice is being given. Sunzi was writing a manual for a warrior king, with most of the content being specific to that context.

With all that said, however, it should be noted that the book is still revered and referred to at the highest levels of policymaking within the government of the People's Republic of China. There is also a whole body of contemporary analyses and commentaries on Sunzi being actively produced under the auspices of the modern People's Liberation Army (PLA) for use by both strategists and active military personnel.

According to long tradition, 兵法 was written by Sun Wu, better known as Sunzi (Sun Tzu in the old-style Romanization), a general and strategist in the service of King He Lü of Wu during the Spring and Autumn Annals period of ancient China (770–476 BCE).

No two interpretations of *The Art of War* are alike. In the translated quotations that follow, I have used one of the most widely accepted versions of the text from the Song Dynasty period (960–1279 CE), and where conflicting interpretations exist, have attempted to allow context and the balance of the prose to dictate my translation.

Each chapter addresses an aspect of organization or strategic planning. What are notable throughout, and what raise the work far above a simple military manual, are the elegance of the prose and the underlying Daoist principles. In the eyes of Sunzi, a general is no mere jobbing soldier: he is a scholar, gentleman and philosopher. The depth of meaning which this element of mysticism imparts is undoubtedly responsible for the work's continuing and universal appeal.

兵者,國大事,死生之地,存亡之道

"Understanding the nature of war is of vital importance to the State. War is the place where life and death meet; it is the road to destruction or survival."

道者,令民于上同意者也,可與之死,可與之生,民不 詭也

"A Moral Compass brings the people
into accord with their ruler
so that they will follow him in life
and in death without fear."

天者,陰陽、
寒暑、時制也

"Heaven encompasses night and day, heat and cold and the changing of the seasons."

地者,高下、 遠近、
險易、 廣狹、
死生也

"Earth encompasses nearness and distance,
ease and hindrance,
wide plains and narrow gorges
– matters of life or death."

將者,智、信、仁、勇、嚴也

"The General must be possessed of wisdom, honesty, benevolence, courage and discipline."

將聽吾計,用之必勝,留之;將不聽吾計,用之必敗,去之

"You should retain those of your generals who heed this advice, for they will be victorious; you should dismiss those who do not, for they will be defeated."

勢者,因利而制權也

"To act according to the situation is to seize the advantage by adapting one's plans."

利而誘之,亂而取之,實而備之,強而避之,

"When your enemy seeks an advantage, lure him further;
if he is in disorder, crush him; if he is organized,
be ready for him; when he is strong, avoid him;"

兵者，詭道也。
故能而示之不能，用而示之不用，近而示之遠，遠而 示之近

"Successful war follows the path of Deception.
Thus when you are able to act, feign incapacity;
when deploying, feign inactivity."

攻其不備，出其不意。此兵家之勝，不可先傳也

"Attack where he is unprepared, appear where you are least expected. Thus you may see that in war, surprise is the key to victory."

夫未戰而廟算勝者,得算多也;未戰而廟算不勝者,得算少也

"A victorious leader plans for many eventualities before the battle; a defeated leader plans for only a few."

多算 勝,少算不勝,而況無算乎!

"Many options bring victory, few options bring defeat, no options at all spell disaster."

其用戰也貴勝,久則鈍兵挫銳,攻城則力屈,久暴師則國 用不足

"In waging war, victory is the prize but, if it is delayed, both troops and weapons are blunted; besieging a city exhausts your strength; a protracted campaign depletes the state's resources."

故兵聞拙速，未睹巧之久也。夫兵久而國利者，未之有也

"Thus, although I have heard of reckless haste in war, I have never seen wise delay. Nor has any state benefitted from prolonging war."

故不盡知用兵之害者，則不能盡知用兵之利也

"Only someone who understands the perils of waging war can also understand the best way of conducting it."

善用兵者,役不再籍,
糧不三載;取用于國,
因糧于敵,故軍食
可足也

"A skilled general levies troops only once and transports provisions from home only twice. He brings equipment from home but forages for food from the enemy; this is how he keeps his troops fed."

國之貧于師者遠輸,遠
輸則百姓貧

"Provisioning an army at a distance is a sure way
of emptying the state exchequer and beggaring the populace."

故殺敵者,怒也;取敵之利者,貨也

"For your soldiers, anger must be the spur to killing the enemy and reward must be the stimulus to defeating them."

故車戰,得車十乘已上,賞其先得者

"Thus in a chariot battle, if ten chariots or more are taken, then reward the soldiers who captured the first one."

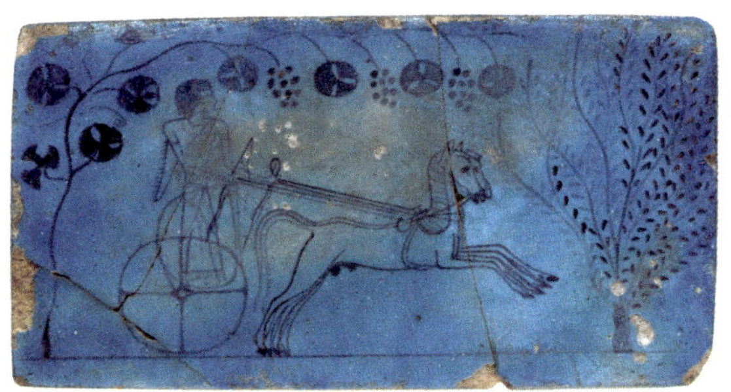

而更其旌旗,車雜而乘之,卒善而養之,是謂勝敵而益強

"Change the flags and standards on the captured chariots and add them to your own squadrons. Treat the captured soldiers well and look after them. This is the tactic of using the defeated enemy to increase your strength."

故兵貴勝，不貴久

"So you can now see that in war it is winning alone that matters and there is no merit in prolonging a campaign."

故知兵之將，民之司命，國家安危之主也

"A general who truly understands warfare controls the people's fate. He is the master of the state's security."

凡用兵之法全國為上,破國次之;

"In considering the complete art of war, it is greatly preferable to capture a state whole rather than break it up."

全軍為上破軍次之

"It is better to capture an army whole rather than break it up."

是故百戰百勝,非善之善也

"Winning a hundred victories out of a hundred battles is not the ultimate achievement…"

不戰而屈人之兵，
善之善者也

"…the ultimate achievement is to defeat the enemy without even coming to battle."

故上兵伐謀,其次伐交,其次伐兵,其下攻城

"Thus it follows that the highest form of warfare is to out-think the enemy. next is to break his alliances; then to defeat his armies in battle; the lowest form is to besiege his cities."

攻城之法為不得已

"Siege warfare should only be undertaken if it is unavoidable."

拔人之城而非攻也,破人之國而非久也,必以全爭于天下,故兵不頓,而利可全,此謀攻之法也

"Thus a skilful general must defeat the enemy without coming to battle, take his cities without a siege and overthrow his state without a long campaign. He must make every effort under Heaven to achieve total victory with his forces undiminished: this is the art of strategic offence."

故用兵之法,十則圍之,五則攻之,倍則分之,敵則能戰之,少則能逃之,不若則能避之

"Thus, when deploying your troops, if you outnumber the enemy ten to one, surround him; five to one, attack him; two to one, split him. If forces are equal, engage him in open battle; if you in turn are slightly outnumbered, evade his advances; if you are heavily outnumbered, withdraw completely."

故小敵之堅

"A smaller force, no matter how determined..."

大敵之擒也

"…will always succumb to a larger one."

夫將者,國之輔也。輔周則國必強,輔隙則國必弱

"The army's commander is the mainstay of the State;
if his support is solid, the State will be strong;
if his support is flawed, the State will be weak."

知道在人数占优和寡不敌众时该怎么做，才能取得胜利

"Knowing what to do both when superior in numbers and when outnumbered, brings victory."

故曰:知己知彼,
百戰不貽

"Thus we may say that if you know yourself
and know your enemy,
you will gain victory a hundred times
out of a hundred."

不知彼而知己，一勝一負；

"If you know yourself but do not know your enemy you will meet one defeat for every victory."

不知彼不知己，每戰必貽

"If you know neither yourself nor your enemy, you will never be victorious."

昔之善戰者,先為不可勝,以待敵之可勝

"The great generals of old first ensured that they themselves were beyond defeat and then waited for the enemy to make themselves vulnerable."

不可勝者,守也;可勝者,攻也

"While you are unsure of victory, defend; when you are sure of victory, attack."

守則不足,攻則有餘

"Defence should indicate that you are not in a position to defeat the enemy, attack that you are even stronger than you need to be."

善守者,藏于九地之下;善攻者,動于九天之上

"A skilled defender digs himself in deeper than the ninth level of the Earth; a skilled attacker falls on the enemy from above the ninth level of Heaven."

戰勝而天下曰善,非善之善者也

"A victory that is acclaimed by all and sundry is by no means the greatest of victories."

古之所謂善戰者,勝于易勝者也

"The great warriors of old not only won victories, but won them with ease."

善用兵者,修道而保法,故能為勝敗之政

"A great strategist follows his Moral Compass and adheres to his methods of Regulation, for these are the means by which he determines victory or defeat."

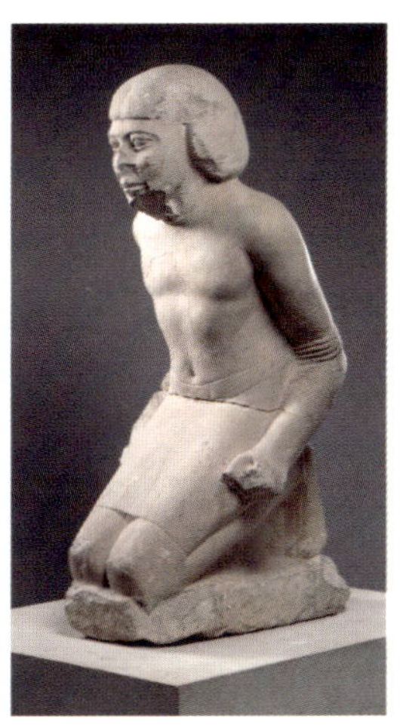

是故勝兵先勝而後求戰，

"A vanquished army will have gone into battle first…"

敗兵先戰而後求勝

"...and only then looked for the means of victory."

兵法:一曰度,二曰量,三曰數,四曰稱,五曰勝

"In the art of war, first comes scoping, then measurement, then calculation, then balancing and finally victory."

地生度,度生量,量生數,數生稱,稱生勝

"The ground is the basis for scoping, scoping the basis for measurement, measurement the basis for calculation, calculation the basis for balancing, and balancing the basis for victory."

勝者之戰民也,若決積水于千仞之谿者,形也

"A victorious army carries all the weight of flood water plunging into a thousand-foot gorge."

三軍之衆,可使
必受敵而無敗,
奇正是也;

"To hold an entire army unbroken in the face of enemy attack is achieved by use of both the oblique and the direct."

兵之所加，
如以碫投卵者，
虛實是也

"To make the force of your army's attack like a grindstone crushing an egg, you must master the substantial and the insubstantial."

凡戰者,以正合,以奇勝

"In all kinds of warfare, the direct approach is used for attack, but the oblique is what achieves victory."

故善出奇者,無窮如天地,不竭如江河

"A general who understands the use of the oblique
has a source of tactics as inexhaustible as Heaven and Earth,
which, like the Rivers and the Oceans, will never run dry."

戰勢不過奇正,奇正之變,不可勝窮之也

"In military strategy, there is only the direct and the oblique, but between them they offer an inexhaustible range of tactics."

激水之疾,至于漂石者,勢也

"The surge of rolling flood-water washes away boulders: this is called momentum."

鷙鳥之疾,至于毀折者,節也

"The swoop of a falcon strikes and kills its prey: this is called timing."

是故善戰者,其勢險,其節短

"Thus for a skilled warrior, his momentum must be irresistible and his timing precise."

亂生于治,怯生于勇,弱生于強

"In this way, apparent confusion masks true organization; cowardice masks courage; weakness masks strength."

治亂,數也;勇怯,勢也;
強弱,形也

"Confusion and organization are a matter of deployment.
Cowardice and courage are a matter of momentum.
Strength and weakness are a matter of formation."

故善戰者,求之于勢,
不責于人

"The skilled general seeks combined momentum and does not rely on individual prowess."

故善戰人之勢,如轉圓石于千仞之山者,勢也

"The momentum of skilled warriors is like a round boulder tumbling down a thousand-foot mountain."

凡先處戰地而待敵者佚

"It is a general principle that the army which arrives first at the site of battle and waits for the enemy will be fresh."

後處戰地而趨戰者勞

"The army that arrives second to the field
and has to rush into battle will
be laboured and exhausted."

我專為一，敵分為十，
是以十攻其 一也，則
我衆而敵寡；

"If you are a single unit but the enemy is divided into ten,
then the odds are ten to one in your favour at any given point."

故善戰者，致人而不致于人

"Thus a great warrior takes control of others and does not let others control him."

出其所不趨,趨其所不意

"Attack at points which the enemy must scramble to defend, and launch lightning attacks where they are not expected."

守而必固者，守其所不攻也

"To be sure in defence, mount your defences at those places the enemy cannot attack."

微乎微乎,至于無形,
神乎神乎,至于無聲,
故能為敵之司命

"Be subtle! You can make yourself invisible.
Be secretive! You can move without a sound.
Thus you hold the enemy's fate in your hands."

進而不可御者,沖其虛也;退而不可追者,速而不可及也

"To advance without the possibility of being checked, you must strike fast at the enemy's weakest points. To retreat without the possibility of being caught, you must march at a speed the enemy cannot match."

我不欲戰,雖畫地而守之,敵不得與我戰者,乖其所之也

"If you do not wish to engage with the enemy, even though your defences are no more than a line in the ground, you can prevent them attacking by luring them away with a feint or a decoy."

故形人而我無形，則我專而敵分

"If you can see the enemy's dispositions, but they cannot see yours, then you can keep your forces united while they must split up to allow for all possibilities."

寡者備人者也，衆者使人備己者也。

"Weakness in numbers stems from having to mount defences; strength in numbers stems from forcing the enemy to mount such defences."

故形兵之極,至于無形;無形,則深間不能窺,智者不能謀

"In deploying your troops, the greatest skill is in keeping the enemy in the dark. Keep your dispositions secret so that the most thorough of searches cannot discover them and they are hidden from the sharpest of intellects."

夫兵形象水，水之形避高而趨下，兵之形，避實而擊虛，水因地而制流，兵應敵而制勝

“Military strategy is like water, which flows away from high ground towards low ground. So, in your tactics, avoid the enemy’s strengths and attack his weaknesses. Water adapts its course according to the terrain; in the same way you should shape your victory around the enemy’s dispositions.”

故兵無常勢,水無常形

"There are no constants in warfare,
any more than water maintains a constant shape."

故五行無常勝，
四時無常位，
日有短長，月有死生。

"None of the Five Elements remains dominant for long;
none of the Four Seasons lasts indefinitely;
the Sun rises and sets; the Moon waxes and wanes.

能因敵變化而取勝者，謂之神

"Thus a general who gains victory by shaping his tactics according to the enemy, ranks with the Immortals."

对敌演习可能带来巨大优势，也可能带来巨大危险

"Manoeuvres against the enemy can bring great advantage or great peril."

如果您等待集结装备齐全的部队再试图夺取优势，您就有可能来得太晚

"If you wait to muster your force with full equipment before trying to seize an advantage, you risk arriving too late."

故兵以詐立,以利動,以分和為變者也

"In warfare, subterfuge is your foundation, advantage your motivation, and circumstance determines your formation."

故其疾如風,其徐如林,侵掠如火,不動如山,難知如陰,動如雷震

"You must be swift as the wind, dense as the forest, rapacious as fire, steadfast like a mountain, mysterious as night and mighty as thunder."

先知迂直之計者勝,此
軍爭之法也

"Victory belongs to him who has mastered the combination of the devious and the direct."

」夫 金鼓旌旗者,所以一人之耳目也;

"Gongs and drums, and banners and flags make the army hear with the same ear and see with the same eye."

是故朝氣銳,晝氣惰,
暮氣歸

"In the morning a soldier is full of fight,
in the afternoon he is slowing down, and in the evening he thinks only of returning to camp."

故善用 兵者,避其銳氣,擊其惰歸,此治氣者也

"A skilled general will avoid the enemy when they are full of fight, and engage with them when their thoughts have turned to their beds. This is mastery of morale."

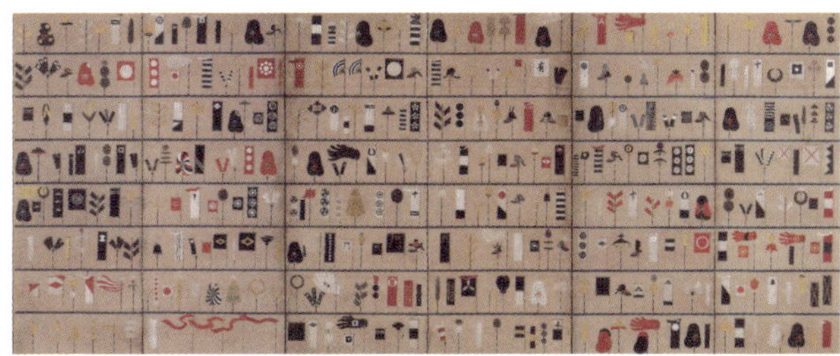

無邀正正 之旗,無擊
堂堂之陣,此治變者也

"Holding off from an enemy whose banners are well ordered, and not engaging with an army in tight formation, this is mastery of circumstance."

餌兵勿食，
歸師勿遏

"Do not swallow the bait put out for you,
and do not get in the way of an army that is homeward bound."

故用兵之法,高陵勿向,背丘勿逆,佯北勿從銳卒勿攻

"Here are some basic principles of war:
never attack uphill, nor defend downhill;
do not be lured into attack by feigned flight,
and do not attack an enemy who is rested and full of fight."

Picture Credits

Alamy: 11 (DC Premiumstock), 13 (Science History Images), 22 (Penta Springs), 23 (Album), 24 (Jim Gibson), 27 (Print Collector), 28 (Rania Hegazi), 30 (Photo 12), 36 (CPA Media), 40 (Classic Image), 45 (James Davis Photography), 49 (Niday Picture Library), 50 (Heritage Image Partnership), 53 (George Robertson), 61 (Album), 68 (Sergi Boixader), 69 (Horst Friedrichs), 73 (Thisimaje DSP - Howard Johnston), 83 (Image Source), 84 (Kevin Archive), 86 (World History Archive), 87 (Roman Kybus), 88 (imageBROKER), 89 (Pictorial Press), 94 (Azoor Prague)

Depositphotos: 6

Dreamstime: 8 (Rawlik), 10 (Zhasminaivanova), 15 (Ermess), 19 (Ronscall1), 20 (Bpperry), 34 (F4f), 35 (Meoita), 39 (Davidemarsden), 41 (Photobyemily), 42 (Jorisvo), 44 (Radiokafka), 48 (Sepavo), 55 (Sadikgulec), 56 (minnystock), 58 (Pinkcandy), 59 (Mountaintreks), 63 (Schlag), 65 (Dudlajzov), 66 (Vladj55), 72 (beibaoke1), 74 (Maloff2), 79 (Artphotokor), 91 (Somatuscani)

J. Paul Getty Museum: 12

LACMA: 25

Library of Congress: 9, 76

Metropolitan Museum of Art, New York: 5, 14, 16, 18, 20, 26, 29, 32, 33, 38, 43, 47, 51, 52, 54, 62, 64, 70, 71, 78, 80, 81, 82, 90

Minneapolis Institute of Art: 93

Public Domain: 17, 31, 37, 46, 85, 92, 95

Shutterstock: 67 (Nataliya Nazarova)

Walters Art Museum, Baltimore: 57, 60, 75, 77